SUPER CITIES!

KANSAS CITY

by **Mark Shulman**

arcadia
CHILDREN'S BOOKS

Published by Arcadia Children's Books
A Division of Arcadia Publishing
Charleston, SC
www.arcadiapublishing.com

First published 2022

Manufactured in the United States.

ISBN 978-1-4671-9856-1

Library of Congress Control Number: 2021943252

Produced by Shoreline Publishing Group LLC
Santa Barbara, California
Designer: Patty Kelley

Contents

Kansas City

Going to Kansas City? There are actually two! These cities sit across the Missouri River from each other. The smaller one is Kansas City, Kansas, but most of the places featured in this book are in the much larger city of Kansas City, Missouri. So when you see "KC," it means Kansas City, MO!

They call KC the "Heart of America." That's not surprising, since the city is almost at the exact center of the continental USA. It's called "The Paris of the Plains" for its many beautiful boulevards, buildings, and thriving arts scene—like Paris, France. And it's called the City of Fountains because, well, it

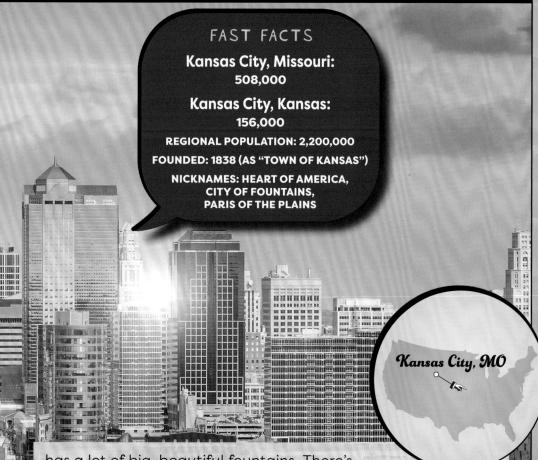

Kansas City, MO

has a lot of big, beautiful fountains. There's nothing plain about this place!

Kansas City has tons of great activities for kids. Love food? Many say the barbecue here is the best. Love sports? The beloved local teams are champions. Love giant badminton birdies? Kansas City has the largest, hands down! Love Walt Disney? This is where his animation magic began.

There's so much natural beauty in Kansas City, too. Parks and plains and waterslides . . . and more. To find out more, just turn the page!

KANSAS CITY: Map It!

Kansas City is the largest city in the state of Missouri. Kansas City, Kansas, is the third-largest city in that state.

The Missouri city began where the Kansas River meets a bend in the Missouri River. Early river travelers stopped here to rest, to trade goods, or to settle down and make a new home. River traffic is still an important part of the region's economy.

Over the years the trains came along, and then highways. Since then, Kansas City has kept growing. Because it's smack-dab in the middle of the country, even if you're not going there, there's a chance you'll be passing through town on your way to somewhere else.

Kansas City, Missouri

IOWA

ILLINOIS

Kansas City

KANSAS

MISSOURI

ARKANSAS

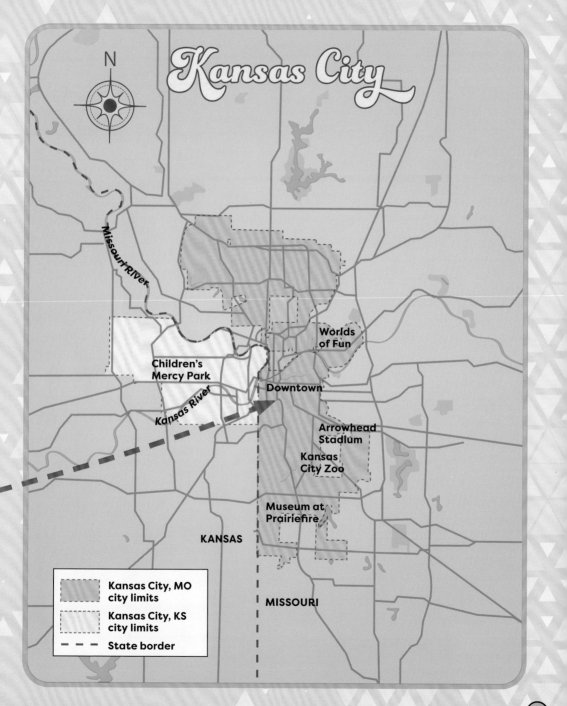

Kansas City

N

Missouri River

Children's
Mercy Park

Kansas River

Worlds
of Fun

Downtown

Arrowhead
Stadium

Kansas
City Zoo

Museum at
Prairiefire

KANSAS

MISSOURI

Kansas City, MO
city limits

Kansas City, KS
city limits

State border

City of Fountains

It's no surprise why Kansas City earned the nickname "City of Fountains"—it has more than 200 of them! The only city in the world with more is Rome, Italy—and it got a 2,000-year head start!

Each KC fountain is unique—fancy or simple, serious or silly, gigantic or pint-sized. Many neighborhoods design and install fountains that represent their communities.

Most are turned off in winter so ice doesn't damage them. Then, each spring, Kansas Citians celebrate Fountain Day, when all the water starts flowing again.

The city's original fountains weren't built just for beauty. They provided drinking water. A fountain that looked like a lion was the first to be installed in 1904. Water spurted from the lion's mouth for people to drink, and collected at the bottom for horses, dogs, and other animals. Check out some of these other impressive fountains throughout the city:

Six firefighters who died on the job are remembered at the **Firefighters Fountain and Memorial**.

Musicians from the Kansas City Symphony have made recordings that play in tempo with the spurting water jets at **Crown Center Square Fountain**. Kids love to play in it!

The **J.C. Nichols Memorial Fountain**, near the Plaza, was built in Paris, later brought to New York, and ended up in KC in 1951.

MARQUEE
EVENT RENTALS
COMMITTED. EVERY DAY. EVERY EVENT.

KANSAS CITY MEANS . . .

How many American states took their names from Native American languages? The answer is 26—that's more than half. Both Kansas and Missouri got their names this way. Kansas comes from the region's Kaw people. Europeans called the Kaw "Akansa" (also Kanza or Kansa). Kansa means "people of the South Wind." Strong winds whip across the prairie here, so the name makes sense.

Across the river, Missouri is named for the Missouria people. They originally called themselves Mishoori, meaning "Wooden Canoe People." That's not surprising for a place criss-crossed with big rivers to travel on!

Monchousia (White Plume), chief of the Kaw in the 1820s

WORLDS OF FUN!

MAMBA

Worlds of Fun

morgan

If you're looking for fun with a capital F, here's an experience that can feel as big as the planet. Worlds of Fun is one of the largest amusement park complexes in the Midwest, with 235 acres (and another 64 acres next door at Oceans of Fun)! What in the world will you find here?

The park was originally based on the famous book by Jules Verne, *Around the World in 80 Days*. Different sections are based on Earth's different continents, like Africa and Asia.

There are seven roller coasters! Choose between high drops, twists, spins, and upside-down rides—or do them all if you're adventurous.

Mamba Lift

Spinning Dragons

Boomerang Coaster

Oceans of Fun

Oceans of Fun was once the world's largest water park. It's still packed with high slides, riptides, river glides, and other wet rides, including one of the world's longest water slides—the Riptide Raceway is 486 feet long!

The region has been home to Native American people for thousands of years. The Hopewell culture began living here more than 2,000 years ago. They were followed by the Mississippian. Then came the Kansa, Missouria, Osage, and Otos peoples.

MONTANA

NORTH DAKOTA

SOUTH DAKOTA

WYOMING

Early 1700s: A French settler named Etienne de Veniard, Sieur de Bourgmont (that's a mouthful!) is the first known European to explore and settle in the area. He married a woman from the Missouri people and made a living by trading furs. He also wrote reports describing the Missouri River and giving it its name. By 1763, Spanish people had joined the French settlers.

NEBRASK

Denver

RADO

KANS

OKLA

NEW MEXICO

William Clark

TEXAS

1803: Emperor Napoleon of France sold the land that includes Kansas and Missouri to the United States. The next year, American explorers Meriwether Lewis and William Clark came through on their famous expedition to map the continent.

Meriwether Lewis

FAST FACT
Possum Trot? Rabbitville?
Those were some of the other names considered for the town that became "Kansas City."

1821: Missouri became a state. (Kansas would not join the Union until 1861).

NNESOTA

IOWA

St. Louis

MISSOURI

MA

ARKANSAS

1825: The U.S. government forced the Kansa and Osage off their land. They were sent to reservations deep in the territory of Kansas. People from about 100 Native American nations still live in the KC area (see page 27).

Kno-Shr, a Kansa chief in 1853

LOUISIANA

New Orleans

This shows the land included in the 1803 Louisiana Purchase, including the 24th state: Missouri.

1831: A group of Latter-Day Saints (also known as Mormons) from New York State arrived and started a small settlement simply called Kansas. Another settlement, begun by Reverend Isaac McCoy, was called Westport, located near the Kansas River.

1853: The "City of Kansas" became official, with a population of about 2,500 people.

1854: Congress passed The Kansas-Nebraska Act, which created official territories with those names. Settlers in each area could decide whether to allow slavery. Next-door Missouri was pro-slavery and wanted Kansas to be too. However, thousands of anti-slavery supporters, called abolitionists, pushed Kansas to ban slavery. Things turned violent and the next several years were known as "Bleeding Kansas."

1861: By this time, the argument over slavery had divided the country and led to the Civil War. Kansas joined the United States as a free state and a member of the Union. Missouri was part of the Confederate States that supported slavery. The war lasted until 1865.

Oldest Bridge crossing the Mo. River at Kansas City, Mo.

1869: The Hannibal River Bridge opened, which let railroads finally cross the Missouri River. This allowed both Kansas Citys to expand in new directions.

The original Hannibal River Bridge was replaced in 1917 with this one, which still stands.

1870s: The city's first stockyard opened in the West Bottoms area, as KC was becoming a major market for cattle and meatpacking. KC was mooo-ving up!

HISTORY: IT'S GROWING UP!

1900s: Big buildings! As people and money flowed into Kansas City, bigger buildings went up. Safer elevators and steel frames made it possible to construct elegant, impressive office towers as high as 16 stories. Some of these early skyscrapers, like the R.A. Long Building and the Scarritt Building, are protected landmarks today.

To celebrate the arrival of electricity in 1907, Kansas City built a huge amusement park named Electric Park to dazzle people.

Kansas City's famous Union Station opened in 1914.

1920s: KC came under the tight control of political boss Tom Pendergast. Boss Tom decided who got elected, what got built, and where the city's money went. He wasn't afraid to break the law to get what he wanted, but it caught up with him. He got very rich, but finally went to jail—for not paying his income taxes.

1930s: Kansas City's original, swinging style of jazz and blues began to spread all over the country. Local musicians Count Basie, Charlie Parker, Mary Lou Williams and others made America's dance music here. Thanks to records and tours, the city soon became world famous as a music center.

1950s: Following World War II, Kansas City went through a second building boom. Now the suburbs were expanding, thanks to the arrival of new highways and lots of cars. Country Club Plaza became the first suburban shopping mall in the world.

People from the Past!

Take a look at some of the people who have helped shape Kansas City's history:

Eliza Burton Conley (1869-1946)

A member of the Wyandot Nation, Conley became a lawyer to protect a cemetery where her ancestors were buried. Developers wanted to buy it and build on it. The case went to the U.S. Supreme Court, and Conley became the first Native American woman to argue before the Court. She lost the case, but the state eventually protected the cemetery.

Harry S Truman (1884–1972)

Born in Lamar, Missouri, America's 33rd president moved to Kansas City in 1920 to go to college. He worked for the Kansas City Star newspaper, then opened (and closed) a men's clothing store—all in two years! He decided to get into politics, becoming a U.S. Senator in 1935, and U.S. vice president in 1945. He became president a few months later, after President Franklin D. Roosevelt died. Truman was reelected in 1948.

William "Count" Basie (1904-1984)

Basie was already a skilled piano player by his teen years. In 1927, he got stranded in Kansas City when he was on tour with a band. Basie decided to stay in the area, and went on to join several swing and jazz bands in KC, perfecting his talent and style at nightclubs all over the city.

Lucile Harris Bluford (1911-2003)

As a journalist and civil rights activist, Bluford worked for 70 years at the Kansas City Call, a newspaper for the African American community. She started as a reporter, and eventually worked her way up to own the paper.

FAST FACT
Here's a man who made his mark: In 1910, Joyce Hall started the company that eventually became Hallmark cards—get it?

Satchel Paige (1906-1982)

One of baseball's greatest all-time pitchers, Paige played for the Kansas City Monarchs of the Negro League. In 1965, at age 59, he became the oldest major league player ever when he pitched three innings of a game with the Kansas City A's.

KANSAS CITY TODAY

Modern Kansas City, Missouri, may be a mid-sized city, but it's a world-class leader in many ways.

High Quality Living: Why is this city on every list of "best places to live?" The jobs are good, the homes are affordable, and the city is beautiful and easy to live in. No wonder the region is growing!

BBQ: KC has world-famous barbecue . . . smoky and saucy and scrumptious! With their food getting so much love, it's not surprising that KC has more barbecue restaurants for its population than any other city!

BAR·B·Q

Great mass transit! Kansas City has created a new system of electric streetcars and buses, connecting the city like never before. And the cost of a ride downtown is . . . free!

Super Highways: Kansas City has more miles of highways, per person, than any other big city in the country. It's also known as the City of Boulevards, with more than 135 miles of big, wide, beautiful roads.

Great Entertainment: The "Paris of the Plains" has big outdoor spaces, cool theaters and museums, and awesome sports teams. There's no shortage of stuff to do!

TICKET

High Tech: Imagine free, super-high-speed Wi-Fi for everyone. Kansas City became the first U.S. city to provide more than three square miles of free service downtown. It's also the first city anywhere to have hooked up its homes to Google's blazing-fast gigabit fiber network.

Kansas City for Everyone

Black History

The African American Heritage Trail commemorates the rich and often painful experiences of Kansas City's Black community. It's a list of historic sites and events that lets visitors experience history where it happened. Sites include 18th and Vine, the center of Black life in the city in the early 1900s; the Gem Theater; the American Jazz Museum; and the Spirit of Freedom Fountain, along with the sites of homes of famous Black people from Kansas City history.

As with most places in the country, the first Black people in the Kansas City area were enslaved. They arrived mainly in the 1850s, just before the Civil War. They got their freedom after the war, with many finding work in the area's stockyards, packing houses, and railroads. By the 1920s, Black residents totaled about 12 percent of the area population. Beginning in those years, Black musicians gave Kansas City—and the world—its brilliant jazz and blues music.

18th and Vine

Kansas City was also one of the first homes of pro baseball's Negro Leagues. Until 1947, Black players were not allowed in Major League Baseball, even though some of the country's greatest players were African American. The Negro Leagues gave them a place to play from 1920 to the 1950s. The Negro Leagues Baseball Museum (page 30) brings this history to life.

Spirit of Freedom fountain

In the 1950s, wealthier families began to move away from the city center. Some of the older neighborhoods grew poorer and more segregated. After civil rights leader Martin Luther King, Jr., was killed in 1968 (in Memphis, Tennessee), KC saw violent riots break out. KC has seen its share of racial unrest since then, including protests and marches in the Black Lives Matter movement. But the community has also come together to honor its rich Black history.

Bob Kendrick, longtime director of the Negro Leagues Baseball Museum

Native American Life in Kansas City

Native American peoples have a long and sometimes painful history in Kansas City. Many tribes were forced off their land and onto reservations in the 1800s. The Wyandot people were forced out of their homeland in Ohio, and were given land in what is now part of Kansas City, Kansas. (Wyandotte County, in this area, is named for them.)

Today, more than 100 tribes or nations are represented among the people living in both Kansas Citys. Their communities and traditions are strong and varied. The Heart of America Indian Center, also called the Kansas City Indian Center, is an important resource in the community. It coordinates events and services for local Native American families.

And everyone in KC can share in local Native American traditions through gatherings, celebrations, and Native Spirit Radio, a weekly show on KKFI that features music from Native Amerian peoples around the country.

KC's Latinx History

The first Latinx settlers in Kansas City were from Mexico. They came to Kansas City in the early 1800s along the Santa Fe Trail, as traders and merchants. By the early 1900s, many Mexican people had moved into jobs on the area's railroads, in the cattle industry, and as seasonal farm workers.

After World War II, more Latinx families arrived, now from Puerto Rico, Colombia, and other Central American nations. Many settled and started businesses and opened restaurants in the Argentine, Westside, and Armourdale neighborhoods. Kansas City celebrates the rich Latinx heritage with festivals throughout the year.

Asian Life in KC

People from countries in Asia make up about three percent of the greater Kansas City population. They come from many countries, especially China, Japan, the Philippines, and India. Many Indian families visit the area's several Hindu, Islamic, and Sikh houses of worship. Emily Weber (right), who represents Kansas City in the Missouri House of Representatives, is the first Asian American woman to hold that job.

KANSAS CITY WEATHER

If you're one of those people who likes to enjoy all four seasons, Kansas City is a great place to be.

Late spring through early fall are the most popular times to visit, since the weather's warm, there's not (usually) a lot of rain, the fountains are spouting, and there's always some festival, street fair, or outdoor activity to enjoy.

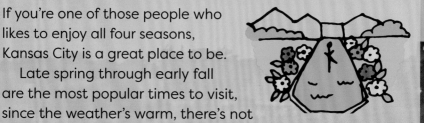

It's not always sunny in Kansas City, but you can count on sunshine about 215 days a year. You'll see rain or snow about 98 days a year. You've probably figured out that doesn't add up to 365, right? Those days are when it's cloudy—but dry!

The hottest month is July, with an average temperature of about 88 degrees, and the coldest is January, with an average of 20 degrees. Those are just averages, though. It can easily top 100 in the summer and go below zero in the winter.

Tornado Alley

Kansas City is on the road to everywhere, and it's right in the middle of this "road." Don't worry too much about ending up like Dorothy from *The Wizard of Oz*, though. The big tornado season is spring, and even then, a direct hit isn't very common. (If you end up in Oz anyhow, say hi to the Scarecrow.)

Buck O'Neil (1911–2006) played with the Kansas City Monarchs. In 1962, he became the first Black coach in Major League Baseball. Later a longtime scout and a founder of the Negro Leagues Baseball Museum, he was elected to the Baseball Hall of Fame in 2022.

The First Negro National League Teams
Chicago American Giants
Chicago Giants
Cuban Stars
Dayton Macros
Detroit Stars
Indianapolis ABCs
Kansas City Monarchs
St. Louis Giants

Things to see in Kansas City

Negro Leagues Baseball Museum

More than one hundred years ago, Black athletes weren't allowed to play in professional baseball. So they formed their own teams. In 1920, eight of these teams were organized in Kansas City as the Negro National League. Today, the Negro Leagues Baseball Museum in the historic 18th and Vine district has sports memorabilia and historic documents that show this era's triumphant and heartbreaking stories.

FAST FACT

Jackie Robinson was a star infielder for the Kansas City Monarchs. He broke baseball's "color line" when he finally was allowed into the Major Leagues with the Brooklyn Dodgers in 1947.

The Other B-Ball

In many places, men's college basketball is just as big-league as the NBA. The College Basketball Experience in KC is that sport's official hall of fame. Games and simulators let you dribble, dunk, report from the broadcast booth, and more.

Things to see in Kansas City

Another side of KC is all the cool stuff for kids to do—you might say KC stands for "Kid Central!"

Union Station

The century-old Union Station still has trains come through, but you don't need to be going "somewhere else" to visit. This magnificent building also houses a number of great family attractions, restaurants, shopping, and more. Go at night to see it all lit up.

- **Planetarium:** An out-of-this-world experience, plus telescope viewings.

- **City Stage Theatre:** Performance space offering live shows of all kinds.

- **Model Train Gallery:** A gigantic world of miniature trains that has great holiday displays.

- **Regnier Extreme Screen Theatre:** Five stories high and 75 feet wide. Need we say more?

Science City

KC's hands-on, interactive Science City in historic Union Station lets kids discover super-cool stuff about the universe! You can dig in at the Dino Dig, "fly" a helicopter, and ride across a very narrow beam on the SkyBike. It's a great way to do some science—without the homework!

Crown Center

Lots of people think of Crown Center as one of the city's "crown jewels." It was built by Hallmark (the company that makes the cards), which is headquartered in Kansas City. There's plenty to do here—eat, shop, play, go to the theater, even ice skate!

Take in a show at the **Coterie Theatre**, which focuses on productions for kids. Also on site is the **MTH Theater**: MTH stands for Musical Theater Heritage, and you guessed it—it's all about musicals and revues.

The **Crown Center Ice Terrace** is open in the winter months for people to strap on some skates and slide around a bit. (Everyone in the same direction, please!)

Young kids especially will have fun at the **LEGOLAND Discovery Center**, where the playground is constructed from giant LEGO blocks. The rule here? All adults must be accompanied by children.

Get creative and make your own art at **Kaleidoscope**, a studio that's run by the Crayola crayons folks.

CENTER
nts • cinemas
GOLAND
COVERY CENTER

Dive in to the **Sea Life Kansas City Aquarium**, where you can "sea" sharks, starfish, seahorses, sea turtles—plus other creatures whose names might not start with "s."

Things to see in Kansas City

You can enjoy the sunshine and people watching in these popular Kansas City gathering spots. Best of all, they're free!

River Market

This historic area is located where Kansas City was first founded. Today, old warehouses have been converted into a trendy area filled with restaurants and shops—but the history is still there. At the heart of River Market is City Market, the largest farmers' market in the region, which has been going strong for more than 150 years. Visitors can shop for local produce, or pick up specialty items that come from around the world.

Power and Light District

Named for an historic Kansas City skyscraper, this place is all lit up with tons of shops and restaurants. There are free concerts and other events throughout the year, and a giant TV makes it a favorite place for folks to come and cheer on sports teams.

Country Club Plaza

Upscale shopping is one of the prime activities on the Plaza, but if you don't have any extra money, that's fine, too. It's just as fun to stroll the streets (or along nearby Brush Creek). There are often street performers or a street fair going on.

Kauffman Memorial Garden

To get away from the bustle, check out the Kauffman Memorial Garden. This 2-acre botanical garden, near the Plaza, has 7,000 plants in five distinct areas, with pathways and seating throughout to take a breather. It's also a great place to see butterflies!

GETTING AROUND

KANSAS CITY

Kansas City is a big place, but thanks to a modern mass transit system called RideKC, it's not too difficult to get around town.

Scooters: Free-wheeling riders who'd rather stand can rent scooters in a number of places. These aren't your typical kiddie scooters. They go really fast!

Streetcars: In 1870, the first streetcars in Kansas City were pulled by horses. Today, the all-electric streetcar system is called KC Streetcar. It runs on rails, and it's free to ride! The two-mile route travels mainly on Main Street, through the central business and entertainment areas. At one end is Union Station; at the other is City Market. There are ten stops in total now, and more are planned for the future.

Buses: The local bus system is reliable and well-used. There are more than 6,500 bus stops spreading across the seven counties (and two states) of greater KC, and some of the new buses are electric, so they run on clean energy.

Bike Sharing: Want to get around on two wheels? RideKC Bike is a popular bike-share program that lets riders choose from good old pedal-powered or all-new electric-assist bikes. You'll find these white bikes—and their orange seats—docked on special bike racks in public spaces all across the region.

IT'S OFFICIAL!

They say a city's not a real city unless it's got "official" things. Who says that? We did! Anyway, here are some of Kansas City's "official" city things.

OFFICIAL SEAL OF KANSAS CITY, MO

The fountain design is for the City of Fountains, of course. The artist chose the blue to represent water and the hot pink to reflect the friendliness of KC residents. This colorful seal was selected in 1991 from among 120 contest entries.

KANSAS CITY
MISSOURI

OFFICIAL FLOWER

The iris blooms in every color of the rainbow. Powell Gardens, near Kansas City, has one of the finest iris collections in North America.

OFFICIAL MINERAL

Galena is a mineral rich in lead ore, a metal that's been used for all kinds of strong, heavy items. Both Kansas and Missouri have made sparkly galena their state mineral.

OFFICIAL MISSOURI STATE STUFF

Dessert: Ice cream cone
Musical instrument: Fiddle
Exercise: Jumping jacks

OFFICIAL BIRD

Since 1927, the Eastern Bluebird has been the official bird of Missouri. But don't let this songbird's name fool you: it's actually red, white, and blue!

Charlie Parker Memorial:
Whose big green head is that in the historic 18th and Vine district? It's a memorial to KC's native son, Charlie Parker. The ten-foot bronze head sits atop an eight-foot base. An alto saxophonist and composer sometimes called "Yardbird" or "Bird," the KC-born Parker led the 1940s Bebop jazz revolution. This was a fast, complex form of jazz made for listening, not dancing. The pioneering Parker influenced many other musicians, including John Coltrane and Ornette Coleman, among others.

BIRD LIVES

Art in Kansas City

Outdoors or indoors, Kansas City has a ton of art to see and enjoy.

Art Alley: In the east end of Kansas City's vibrant Crossroads Arts District, you'll find Art Alley. The area's old brick buildings feature diverse—and always changing—murals and wall art. First Fridays: On the first Friday evening of each month, everything stays open late and visitors can check out new art at the area's galleries.

Sky Stations: These four 200-foot-high towers, designed in a 1930s art deco style, stretch above the Bartle Hall Convention Center. Lights on top can be seen for two miles at night!

Bull Wall: Back in its early days, Kansas City had more livestock than people. The cattle weren't just for dinner. The Bull Wall, created by local artist Robert Morris, commemorates the city's tradition of rodeos and livestock shows. It's a 120-foot long steel wall, with 15 full-size cutouts of running bulls.

Great Museums

The National Museum Of Toys And Miniatures claims "the world's largest collection of fine-scale miniatures." In other words: fancy, dollhouse-sized furniture set in ultra-detailed historic interiors, from a teeny recreation of a Versailles palace room (Versailles is a huge palace in France) to a tiny 1900s architect's classroom.

The four giant birdies outside the Nelson-Atkins were made by Claes Oldenburg and are about 18 feet high.

Kemper Museum of Contemporary Art: On the outside, you'll notice the building's modern design, with its funky sloping metal roof (plus, a giant, creepy spider!). The inside is packed with wonderful, whimsical—and sometimes weird—modern art. The collection includes pieces from famous American artists like Georgia O'Keeffe, Jackson Pollock, and William Wegman. Inside and out, the building is one fun destination. (Except maybe that spider!)

At the **Nelson-Atkins Museum**, giant shuttlecocks—those little birdies used in badminton—are the welcome mat for a beautiful, classic Greek-style temple of art. Inside, you'll find more than 42,000 pieces representing the world and its cultures. You'll find art from world-famous artists such as Monet, Van Gogh, and Noguchi. The Asian art collection (right) is one of the largest in the United States.

More Great Museums

Museum at Prairiefire: Go back into the ancient past to create your own prehistoric creature, explore missions to space, check out the Discovery Center, and visit preserved wetlands at this huge and gorgeous museum that focuses on science, culture, art, and natural history.

The Money Museum: First the good news: All visitors will take home a free bag of real dollar bills from the Money Museum, which is located in the Federal Reserve Bank of Kansas City. Lift a 27-pound gold bar, see the Harry S Truman coin collection, and enjoy displays that explain all about U.S. money. Now the bad news: The money you get will be a bag of old bills that have been shredded into confetti. What did you expect for free?

National Airline History Museum: Inside an old airline hangar, the National Airline History Museum explores Kansas City's rich history as a central hub of several airlines. Five vintage aircraft are on display, along with the 22-foot-tall, 1956 Moonliner II, a reproduction of an original Disneyland ride. There are also flight simulators you can try out.

The Steamboat *Arabia*: In 1856, a riverboat called the steamboat *Arabia* sank in the Missouri River near Kansas City. It wasn't pulled out until 1988! Onboard were 200 tons of cargo, enough to fill a museum—and now it does. The Arabia Steamboat Museum is packed with all kinds of everyday items: tools, guns, toys, household supplies, and even a jar of very, very old pickles. For 132 years, the cool waters of the river kept everything, including the boat, in perfect condition!

Performing Arts

You can catch a show or some live music at one of Kansas City's many theaters and performance halls—or at one of the festivals held throughout the year (see pages 84-85). Here are some popular spots:

Kauffman Center for Performing Arts: This is the main place to see music, dance, opera, theater, and more. It's home to the city's symphony, ballet company, and opera. It opened in 2011 and includes two large theater spaces and a huge lobby that hosts events, too.

FAST FACT
Muriel McBrien Kauffman was the key person behind building the center. Her family also owned the Kansas City Royals for a long time.

Starlight Theatre: Watch performers act, sing, and dance under the stars! Traveling Broadway shows and top concert acts are among the shows you can see here.

The Music Hall: This massive building opened in 1936; its outside is classic Art Deco architecture. See performances by the symphony and other large musical groups here.

Folly Theater: This downtown landmark is more than 100 years old. It's been fixed up to be comfortable for modern audiences, and is a great place to see jazz concerts, performances for children, and live theater.

ING ARTS

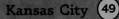

How to Talk Kansas City

Kansas City folks say things their own way. It won't be too long before you'll hear some of these words.

Pop
A soft drink that nobody ever calls "soda."

RAISED ROYAL
How were you raised? In Kansas City, the only way to do it right is to create Royals baseball fans!

Burnt Ends
The best part of a barbecue brisket, and a delicacy that started in KC.

Super Flea
A giant flea market.

KAY SEE MO AND JO CO
Nicknames for Kansas City, Missouri (get it?) and Johnson County.

Missourah
Your teacher might pronounce the state's name as Missour-ee, but locals say Missour-ah.

KAW

What locals call the Kansas River.

Mizzou

The University
of Missouri

The K

Kauffman Stadium, home
of the Kansas City Royals.

Moo U

Kansas City University,
where many students
study agriculture.

**POWER & LIGHT,
OR JUST "P&L"**

A downtown food and
entertainment district.

KANSAS CITY: It's Weird!

Who are you calling weird? Maybe we should just say some things are a little . . . different in Kansas City. Here are some examples:

Leila's Hair Museum
What's so weird about jewelry, wreaths, and other objects? Well . . . at Leila's Hair Museum in nearby Independence, Missouri, they're all made of human hair! But it's not just any hair. They've got the lock on locks from Marilyn Monroe, Michael Jackson, four U.S. presidents, and England's Queen Victoria. Better hurry—it could be hair today, gone tomorrow!

The Boy and Frog Fountain
This fountain, installed in 1929, has made quite a splash. The pedestal features a faun riding a dolphin, while up above, a very happy toddler faces a little frog. No matter what it may look like, the water absolutely squirts from the frog onto the boy. Got it?

FAST FACT
Kansas City has the world's oldest waterbed store!

The 1950s All-Electric House

Once upon a time capsule, people flocked to see this all-electric house of the future! When the Kansas City Electric Company built this ranch-style model home in 1954, visitors were impressed with its electric curtain openers, garage door openers, a hidden TV, and air conditioning. It's also got vintage '50s furniture and products inside. Find it now in the Johnson County Museum in nearby Overland Park, Kansas.

Subtropolis

Billed as "the world's largest underground business complex," Subtropolis is a massive warehouse mined from a limestone cave more than 100 feet below Kansas City's surface. It has eight-and-a-half miles of roads!

Kansas City Workhouse

The abandoned castle on Vine Street was the old Kansas City Workhouse, where small-time criminals once did public work instead of going to jail. After closing in 1972, it became a hot spot for graffiti artists. Even weirder—if the workhouse were still operating, that's where convicted graffiti artists probably would go! It's abandoned now, but plans always pop up for restoration.

What People Do IN KANSAS CITY

If you lived in Kansas City in the 19th century, there weren't too many job choices. You could be a farmer, a railroad worker, or someone who raised or processed cattle. But now, in the 21st century, there's more to KC than raising and moving meat.

Greetings! Hallmark, the giant greeting card publisher, is headquartered here.

Healthcare: Kansas City hospitals, and the region's many connected healthcare providers, are big employers.

Transportation: In addition to railroad and river traffic, Kansas City is a leader in trucking, warehousing, and logistics, which means arranging how trucks and warehouses connect.

Technical services: Two giant cell phone companies—Sprint and T-mobile—merged in 2020. Their main offices are in the KC suburb of Overland Park, Kansas. Not far away, Cerner is a tech leader for the healthcare industry.

Many famous people have called Kansas City home. Here are a few of them.

Janelle Monae (Born 1985)
This Kansas City native learned to sing in church, and launched her hip-hop career with a self-released demo album when she was only 17 years old! She's gone on to record several more albums and win awards for her music. She's also been in TV shows and starred in the hit movie *Hidden Figures*, about African American women who worked for NASA and were critically important to the success of the first manned flight into orbit.

Eminem (Born 1972)
The hip hop artist and producer Eminem, one of the world's top-selling artists, was born Marshall Mathers in St. Joseph, Missouri, just north of Kansas City. He entered the rap scene with the 1999 album *The Slim Shady*, and quickly became an international rap star. Eminem has won 15 Grammy awards, and two of his albums became the worldwide bestselling albums of the year.

Paul Rudd (Born 1969)

The actor in Marvel's Ant-Man moved to the Kansas City area when he was 10. He went to Shawnee Mission West High School, and then studied theater at the University of Kansas, in nearby Lawrence, Kansas. Rudd later founded The Big Slick, a charity event where celebrities and sports stars join to benefit Kansas City's Children's Mercy Hospital.

Don Cheadle (Born 1964)

Marvel Universe movies love Kansas City's actors. Cheadle plays War Machine, one of Iron Man's best friends. He's had many other movie and TV roles, and been nominated for many awards. Cheadle was born in KC, before his family moved around the country.

Sean Malto (Born 1989)

This world-renowned professional skateboarder started his career shredding the flat prairielands of nearby Lansing, KS. He was supported early on by Escapist Skateboarding, a locally owned shop in KC. He's since won many events, and has appeared in videos and video games.

Walt Disney's Kansas City

Walt wasn't born in KC, but if he hadn't lived there, he might never have discovered animation. Decide for yourself!

Walt Disney

Home Sweet Home
Walt's family moved to this house at 3028 Bellefontaine in 1910, when he was nine.

Drawing Lessons
Hoping to be an illustrator, Walt took art classes at the Kansas City Art Institute on Saturday mornings. At home, he drew funny animals, using library books as reference.

Professional Artist (at last)

In 1919, Walt got a job drawing ads for a Kansas City ad agency, where he met his early partner, Ub Iwerks. They soon left to start their own art business. It failed in six weeks.

Moving Pictures

In 1920, the Kansas City Film Ad company hired both men to make cartoon ads for movie theaters. But Walt wanted to create short, funny cartoons, using a type of animation called cel animation, where he could draw individual pictures. He left the company to start another business.

The First Disney Cartoons

Walt called this animation studio Laugh-O-Grams. The studio's building is at 1127 E. 31st Street. Future animation superstars Friz Freleng, Carman Maxwell, and Hugh and Fred Harman joined as artists. The company's short cartoons were funny, but not popular enough to keep the studio in business. They closed in 1923 and Walt moved to Hollywood, California.

Even after more failures, Walt stuck it out. He brought Ub Iwerks and other KC artists to Hollywood. He finally broke through when Mickey Mouse first appeared in 1928. And so the magic began!

Eat the Kansas City Way

Kansas City is a food-lover's paradise. Come ready to eat, because the smells are incredible, the tastes are delicious, and the servings can be gigantic!

Tater Tots: KC fans are serious about which diner's tots are best. Eat 'em plain, or try one of the many gourmet versions that can get much bigger—call them tater teens! They can be stuffed with meat, cheese, or anything else.

Puppy Chow: Sorry, Rover, this isn't for you. It's baked Chex cereal mixed with chocolate chips and/or candy, butter, and sugar. Locals use food coloring and candy so colors will match their favorite teams or holidays.

Barbecue!: KC has a world-class reputation for its amazing barbecue. Here's how it's done: Using a dry rub of spices and seasonings, the meat is smoked sloooowly over different kinds of wood. Hours later, the chef adds a thick, usually tomato-based barbecue sauce that can be spicy, sweet, or something in between.

The Skyscraper: Winstead's Steakburgers is famous for—its milkshake! This half-gallon (64-ounce) brain freeze comes in a foot-high vase with your choice of toppings. Good luck finishing it.

Cheesy Corn: This side dish is almost as beloved as the barbecue it's usually served with. In addition to everything in its name, there's usually bacon, cream cheese, and a lot of butter.

Taking the Field!

Folks in Kansas City LOVE their sports teams, filling stadiums and ballparks to cheer them on.

Patrick Mahomes

KANSAS CITY CHIEFS

Joined the American Football League as the Dallas Texans in 1960. Became the Kansas City Chiefs in 1963. Joined the NFL in 1970.

Won the 1962 AFL title as the Texans. The Chiefs won Super Bowl IV after the 1969 season, and Super Bowl LIV after the 2019 season, beating the San Francisco 49ers.

Cool Stuff: When their home stadium is filled, it looks like a sea of red, as most fans wear that team color.

Big Names: Len Dawson, Derrick Thomas, Tony Gonzalez, Patrick Mahomes, Travis Kelce, Tyreek Hill

Home: Arrowhead Stadium

KANSAS CITY ROYALS

Joined the American League in 1969 as an expansion team.

Won the 1985 World Series against a Missouri rival, the St. Louis Cardinals.

Beat the New York Mets to win the 2015 World Series.

Cool Stuff: The Royals' home ballpark features a huge fountain behind center field—seems natural in the City of Fountains!

Big Names: George Brett, Willie Wilson, Amos Otis, Alex Gordon, Sal Perez

Home: Kauffman Stadium

KC CURRENT

Joined the National Women's Soccer League in 2021.

An earlier NWSL team, FC Kansas City, moved to Utah in 2017 after winning the league title twice.

Players from the team also play for five different national teams around the world.

Cool Stuff: The Current announced plans to build the first soccer-only stadium in the NWSL. It will be in the Berkley Riverfront area in Downtown Kansas City.

Big Names: Jéssica Silva, Rachel Corsie, Adrianna "AD" French

Home: Children's Mercy Park (for now!)

Adrianna "AD" French

Johnny Kelly

SPORTING KANSAS CITY

Joined Major League Soccer in 1996

Won the MLS Cup in 2000 and 2013.

Cool Stuff: They have had three names! They started as the KC Wiz, became the KC Wizards, and then changed to Sporting KC starting in 2011.

Big names: Graham Zusi, Matt Besler, Preki, Dom Dwyer, Tony Meola, Johnny Kelly

Stadium: Children's Mercy Park in Kansas City, Kansas

Take it Outside

It's not just pro athletes who get to play in Kansas City. Regular folks enjoy golf, tennis, hiking, biking, water activities, and more.

Active folks make good use of the Indian Creek Bike and Hike trail in **Santa Fe Commons Park**. Take one of the short loop trails or the whole 23-mile winding, watery, wonderful trail system.

Miles of paths and roadways wind along the Missouri River waterfront, giving hikers and bikers plenty of views. **Ermine Case Junior Park** and **Kaw Point Park** sit across from each other where the Kansas and Missouri Rivers meet up. Kayakers and other boating fans can launch from either park.

One great place to hike is the **Ernie Miller Nature Center** in Olathe, Kansas. (part of the Greater KC area). You can also see live animal displays and other exhibits about the region's wildlife.

A Day at the Lake

Soak up the sun, take a swim, paddle around, go fishing—or all of the above—at one of the many lakes in the KC area.

Waterskiing, windsurfing, and power boating are all popular at **Longview Lake** in Kansas City. There's also a swimming beach and water park, as well as softball, golf, and a horse park in the adjacent area.

Lake Jacomo in Blue Springs, Missouri, is a hot spot for boating, windsurfing, and stand-up paddleboarding. It's also open for fishing, and you can camp overnight.

You won't get in anyone's way at **Smithville Lake** in Smithville, Missouri, on the northern side of the city. It's got 7,200 acres, room enough for all! You can swim, boat, and fish, as well as enjoy landlubber activities like hiking, biking, and golf.

COLLEGE TOWN

The Kansas City region offers educational opportunities for students from the local area, and around the world.

UNIVERSITY OF MISSOURI, KANSAS CITY

Founded 1933
Students: 16,000+
Popular majors: business, health, medicine and dentistry, law, humanities
Fast Fact: UMKC is the largest four-year university in the KC area.

PARK UNIVERSITY

Founded 1875
Students: 15,300
Popular majors: business management, psychology, computer science, criminal justice
Fast Fact: Park students built historic Mackay Hall, with its distinctive Gothic stone towers, in the late 1800s.

Kansas City Art Institute

ROCKHURST UNIVERSITY

Founded 1910

Students: 3,000

Popular majors: Health professions, business management and marketing, biomedical sciences, religion, psychology.

Fast Fact: A Jesuit Catholic university, Rockhurst emphasizes public service: graduates get two transcripts, one for academics and the other for community service.

JOHNSON COUNTY COMMUNITY COLLEGE

Founded 1969

Students: 18,300

Popular majors: liberal arts, business administration, health professions, marketing

Fast Fact: Galileo's Pavilion is an environmentally friendly building on campus that has "living walls" made from plants.

KANSAS CITY ART INSTITUTE

Founded 1885

Students: 700

Popular majors: art history, animation and filmmaking, graphic design, painting, creative writing

Fast Fact: Walt Disney took his first formal art lessons here.

LOL!

Kansas City (Etc.) Jokes

Here are some jokes for you to enjoy, all based on things in the Paris of the Midwest!

What are the biggest birds in Missouri?

The Nelson-Atkins badminton birdies!

What sports team is made up of great cooks?

The Kansas City Chefs!

What is the favorite sports team of every King and Queen?

The Kansas City Royals.

Why are KC folks happy to see newcomers move to town?

Because Missouri loves company.

What did the sad graduate say as she left the University of Missouri?

I'll Mizzou you!

Why are there so many bridges over the Kansas and Missouri rivers?

They keep the cars from getting wet!

GO TO THE PARK!

Kansas City has 221 parks to choose from, but the biggest by far is **Swope Park**, right in the middle of the city. It covers 1,805 acres—that's more than double New York City's famous Central Park. You'll find playgrounds, picnic areas, wide-open grass, and trails galore. Or if you want a walk in the woods, there's a big forest, too.

Thomas Swope, a real estate baron, donated the land to Kansas City in 1896.

The park's huge outdoor venue, the Starlight Theatre, seats more than 8,000 people.

Come play or watch soccer on nine fields at the Swope Soccer Village sports complex.

Get in the swing of things on Swope's tennis courts, baseball diamonds, and a championship-sized golf course.

Zip through the trees on the Go Ape Zipline and Adventure Park.

Watch the animals at the Kansas City Zoo on the north side of the park (read more on pages 76-77).

It's Alive! Animals in Kansas City

Keep your eyes open for some of the city's wildlife—and no, we're not talking about the sports fans!

Snakes Alive! S-s-s-s-so you seriously don't like snakes? S-s-s-s-sorry! Several species of slithering serpents call KC home. Are you wondering if some of them are venomous? S-s-s-s-sure! Just avoid the Osage copperhead and the timber rattlesnake! S-s-s-s-stay away!

River Rovers In addition to fish and other underwater dwellers, the Kansas and Missouri rivers are home to river otters, muskrats, and beavers. You'll also find coypu (also called nutria), a large, invasive water rodent that was brought from South America in the 1800s for its fur.

They Fly by Night When the sun goes down, bats emerge from their daytime sleeping quarters in caves, under bridges, and in dense wooded areas. The most common are the little brown bat and big brown bat (guess what they look like!) There also red bats and hoary bats.

Prairie Home Companions KC's green spaces are home to lots of small mammals like woodchucks, woodrats, moles, voles, opossum, chipmunks, squirrels, and raccoons. There isn't much open prairie left around Kansas City, but in some less developed areas, you might catch a glimpse of prairie dogs. Also making a little home on the prairie is our favorite-named creature: the lesser prairie chicken. As you might guess, it's smaller than the greater prairie chicken. They're some funny-looking birds.

Big and Bigger Not far from town, in the woods and on the plains, you'll find deer, coyotes, and maybe even a bobcat. Years ago, black bears roamed the area, and occasionally someone still spots one of these predators. Most wild elk and bison herds are gone, although some still live several hours away in the plains areas of Kansas.

WE SAW IT AT THE ZOO

In 1907, the Kansas City Zoological Gardens were planned to be the nation's largest zoo. In 1909, it opened in Swope Park with three monkeys, four lions, a wolf, and little else. At least it was a start!

The zoo grew, and today, it features 1,700 animals, with everything from up-close animal experiences to a new Discovery Center!

Tiger

Penguin

Lions

Lorikeet

Oryx

Go on Safari!

The KC Zoo is known for its collection of African animals, which is one of the nation's best. Take a boat or a sky tram to get an up-close look.

KANSAS CITY BY THE NUMBERS

Stats and facts and digits . . . galore! Here are some of the numbers that make Kansas City what it is.

142.2

Decibels (sound level)
reached at Arrowhead Stadium in 2014, making it the planet's LOUDEST stadium. That's about as loud as a jet engine!

15

Number of bridges spanning the Missouri and Kansas rivers.

4

Number of presidents who have eaten at Arthur Bryant's, the city's most famous barbecue restaurant

100+

Number of barbecue restaurants

60

Number of firefighting-related patents received by George Hale, the KC fire chief from 1882 to 1902 (All hail Hale!)

Made in KC

The McDonald's Happy Meal was invented in Kansas City when an advertising man saw his son reading a cereal box.

The very important-sounding Midwest Research Institute perfected a very important process in the early 1950s—putting the candy coating on M&M's.

The first car bumper stickers rolled off the press in KC in 1946, when a local printer found a way to use extra adhesive paper and fluorescent paint.

134

Miles of trails throughout the city

Spooky Sights

The **Hotel Savoy**, a landmark of KC history, opened in 1888. Its guests have included presidents, business giants, celebrities—and ghosts. For more than a century, people have reported seeing a ghostly man (more likely a past resident than a past president). There is also a little girl dressed in 19th century clothes. The hotel was renovated and reopened in 2018 with a new name— 21c Museum Hotel Kansas City. Most of the hotel moved into the 21st century—but the ghosts haven't gotten the memo.

The **Uriah Epperson House** is a large, rambling 1920s estate home that doesn't look haunted, but how else to explain the following reports: organ music, footsteps, a ghostly woman in an elegant dress, and an unattached arm (dressed in blue) that turns on a light?

Not only is the **John Wornall House** among KC's oldest houses, many say it's among the most haunted. It is a former Civil War hospital, and people claim they have seen Civil War soldiers wander inside and out, then quickly vanish. They say if you pay attention in the children's bedroom, you can hear a rocking chair.

Is **Stull Cemetery**, about an hour west of Kansas City, really haunted, or were the reports just a college prank? Either way, rumors of ghosts, demons, and other "mysterious forces" have caused many to come on Halloween to see for themselves if this old graveyard really is home to spirits.

Every Year!

Here's a look at some of the big events that happen in Kansas City just about every year.

Barbecue Battles: Who has the best sauce? Who makes the tastiest ribs? Who can blow the judges away? Grab a handful of napkins and find out at this annual contest to choose the best BBQers in Kansas at the Great Lenexa BBQ Battle in June. In September, dig into the American Royal World Series of Barbecue that crowns the national champs.

KC Riverfest: Usually held on the Fourth of July, this day-long event features food, music, and fun, ending with fireworks over the Missouri River.

Celebration at the Station: Combining the historic location of Union Station with the crowd-pleasing sounds of the Kansas City Symphony and other performers, this event, usually held on Memorial Day weekend, gets summer off to a star-spangled start.

Fountain Day: It moves around the calendar a bit, but every spring, Kansas City's public fountains all get turned on at once.

Hoop It Up!: College basketball is a very big deal in the Midwest. The best men's and women's teams in the Big 12 conference play their annual championship tournament in March in Kansas City's T-Mobile Arena downtown. Teams from Kansas and Missouri often compete.

 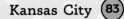

ACROSS THE BORDER

If you walk west across State Line Road, you not only leave Kansas City, Missouri . . . you leave Missouri! You'll be in Kansas City, Kansas (sometimes called KCK). The two Kansas Citys are so connected they sometimes feel like one big city. Here's a look at some of the things you can do and see "across the border." Don't worry—they won't ask for your passport!

Kansas Speedway: Super-fast cars hit the 1.5-mile track for races in NASCAR and other series. When the cars are at top speed, the noise is awesome! Speed fans, check it out!

Spicin Foods: Do you like spicy hot, tongue-busting, eye-watering spicy food? This place sells hot sauces for everything from barbecue to pasta and more. Good luck!

Kaw Point Park: The original name for the Kansas River was the Kaw. This state park was a campsite for the famous Lewis and Clark expedition way back in June 1804. The concrete blocks on display represent the members of the expedition.

Avenue of Murals: Lining Minnesota Avenue is a series of eight murals created by local artists connected to different community groups—Wyandot, Hmong (pictured), African-American, Mexican, and others.

Not Far Away

There's more to explore beyond Kansas City. Here are some great attractions to see that are less than a day (or so) away.

Hi! How's it going? I wanted to tell you about some trips we made. Our first stop was very colorful.

Do you mean you used crayons?

LOL! No, we went to an awesome place filled with flowers: **Powell Gardens**. Check it out!

Wow, that's beautiful!

Yup. There were seven gardens in all. And only 15 minutes from downtown!

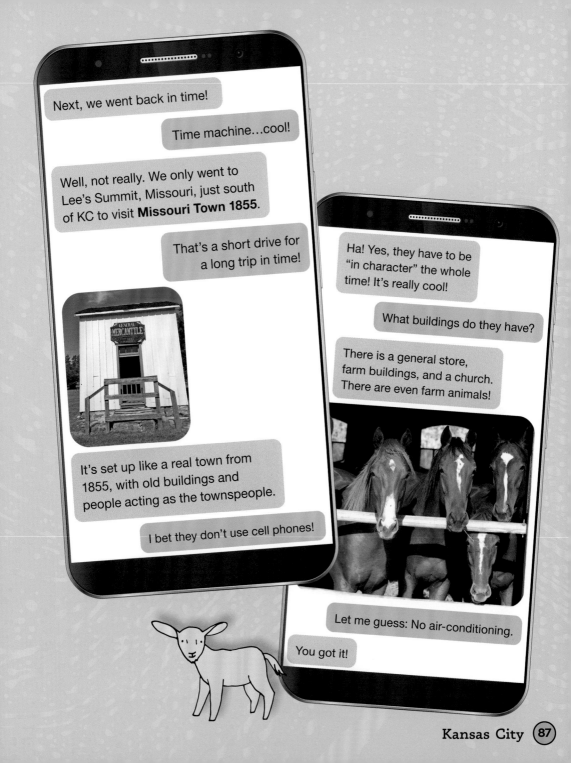

Next, we went back in time!

Time machine…cool!

Well, not really. We only went to Lee's Summit, Missouri, just south of KC to visit **Missouri Town 1855**.

That's a short drive for a long trip in time!

It's set up like a real town from 1855, with old buildings and people acting as the townspeople.

I bet they don't use cell phones!

Ha! Yes, they have to be "in character" the whole time! It's really cool!

What buildings do they have?

There is a general store, farm buildings, and a church. There are even farm animals!

Let me guess: No air-conditioning.

You got it!

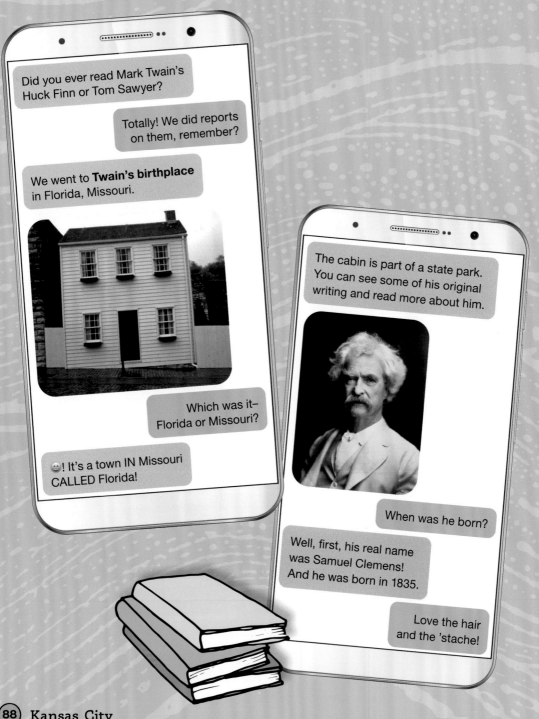

Did you ever read Mark Twain's Huck Finn or Tom Sawyer?

Totally! We did reports on them, remember?

We went to **Twain's birthplace** in Florida, Missouri.

Which was it– Florida or Missouri?

😀! It's a town IN Missouri CALLED Florida!

The cabin is part of a state park. You can see some of his original writing and read more about him.

When was he born?

Well, first, his real name was Samuel Clemens! And he was born in 1835.

Love the hair and the 'stache!

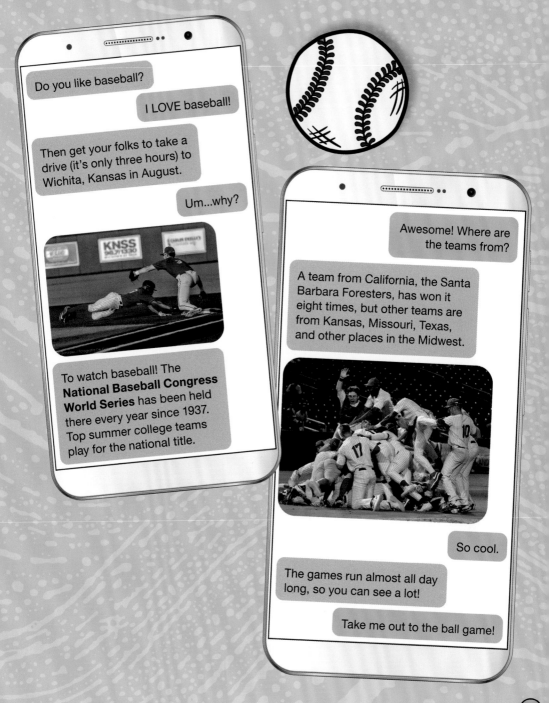

Do you like baseball?

I LOVE baseball!

Then get your folks to take a drive (it's only three hours) to Wichita, Kansas in August.

Um...why?

To watch baseball! The **National Baseball Congress World Series** has been held there every year since 1937. Top summer college teams play for the national title.

Awesome! Where are the teams from?

A team from California, the Santa Barbara Foresters, has won it eight times, but other teams are from Kansas, Missouri, Texas, and other places in the Midwest.

So cool.

The games run almost all day long, so you can see a lot!

Take me out to the ball game!

Sister Cities Around the World

Did you know that a city can have a sister? Kansas City has 13 of them! Since the 1950s, American cities have created official connections with other cities around the globe. They partner up in different areas, from culture to education to business. Let's visit some of Kansas City's sister cities.

Metz, France

Hannover, Germany

Guadalajara and Morelia, Mexico

Seville, Spain

Ramla, Israel

Kurashiki, Japan

Xi'an, China

Tainan, Taiwan

Freetown, Sierra Leone

Port Harcourt, Nigeria

Arusah, Tanzania

Kansas City Sister Cities

Sister Cities in Action

Here are some examples of how Kansas City is working with and helping its sister cities:

Port Harcourt: Kansas City has developed strong connections between its academic and medical institutions and this large African city.

Ramla: Kansas City and Ramla created a program called "Let the Children Play." Kansas City families collected toys that were sent to Muslim and Jewish children in this Israeli city.

Seville: When historic Seville hosted the 1992 World's Fair, Kansas City was the only U.S. city invited!

Hannover: The University of Missouri–KC collaborates with this large industrial city in areas as diverse as music and engineering.

FIND OUT MORE!

Books, Websites, and More!

Books

Bailer, Darice. *What's Great About Kansas? (Our Great States).* Lerner Publications, 2015.

Heinrichs, Ann. *Kansas (U.S.A. Travel).* The Child's World, 2018.

Kelley, K.C. *Kansas City Royals*. Child's World, 2019.

Ortler, Brett. *Backyard Science & Discover Workbook: Midwest.* Adventure Publications, 2021.

Shulman, Mark. *Kansas City Chiefs.* Kaleidoscope, 2020.

Web Sites

https://www.visitkc.com
> The Missouri city's official tourism site.

https://www.visitkansascityks.com
> All about the Kansas City in Kansas!

https://www.ifamilykc.com
> Tons of ideas for kids and families.

https://www.kchistory.org
> A site packed with pictures, artwork, and stories from the city's past.

Photo Credits and Thanks

Photos from Dreamstime, Shutterstock, or Wikimedia unless otherwise noted. 27: EmilyforMissouri.com. AP Photos: Matty Zimmerman 21; Charlie Reidel 25, 30; Susan Pfannmuller/Kansas City Star 85B. Newscom: David R. Frazier/DanitaDelmont.com 13; AdMedia/Splash News/Newscom 57B; Randy Litzinger/Icon Sportswire 64; Serena S.Y. Hsu/Zumapress 65.

Artwork: Lemonade Pixel; others from Shutterstock. Maps (6-7): Jessica Nevins.

Thanks to our pals Nancy Ellwood, Kait Leggett, and the fine folks at Arcadia!

 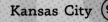

Thanks for Visiting
KANSAS CITY
Come Back Soon!